MARC GAEDE

IMAGES FROM THE SOUTHWEST

1. The Lower Valley, Monument Valley, Utah 1984

Marc Gaede

MARC GAEDE

IMAGES FROM THE SOUTHWEST

Essay by David Lavender

Foreword by Bruce Babbitt

NORTHLAND PRESS
FLAGSTAFF, ARIZONA

 ISBN 0-87358-414-7 CLOTH. ISBN 0-87358-416-3 SOFTCOVER. LIBRARY OF CONGRESS CATALOG CARD NUMBER 86-60517. COMPOSED AND PRINTED IN THE UNITED STATES OF AMERICA.

For Marnie

2. Canyons in Canyon de Chelly, Arizona 1978

FOREWORD

Bruce Babbitt

"Photographs don't lie," author Lawrence Clark Powell said, "they just don't tell the truth." However, that conveyance is greatly influenced by such intangibles as how much the image resembles reality and how closely the emotions of the viewer and the photographer are matched. People tend to see in them what they want to see, and, consequently, to feel what they want to feel. Marc Gaede has taken advantage of that tendency by first stripping his images of all excess, and then infusing them with powerful moods that still allow their viewers room to wander at will emotionally.

For me, these photographs of the Southwest say something about the loss of the old ties between the people of the region and their land. Signs of this profound change are on all sides. Only a generation ago, almost everyone made a living by farming, ranching, or mining. Today, almost everyone lives in a city, doctoring, lawyering, making microchips, and serving fast food. Three of four Arizonans live in Phoenix and Tucson, eighty percent of Utah's population is clustered beneath the Wasatch Front, and sixty percent of Colorado's people live along the Front Range. The gold and silver towns are dead and the copper towns are dying. In Jerome, where 15,000 miners and their families once prospered, a few hundred artists live like gypsies in the ruins of the past. Up in the plateau country, thousands of Navajo Indians are being hustled off the land by government agents from Washington. Up and down old Route 66, promoters are breaking up the cattle ranches and selling them off in 40-acre mail-order promotions. Canadians have been looking at the million-acre Boquillas Ranch as the site for a Bible City modeled after certain family theme parks. And, closer to my own heart, the old summer headquarters of my grandfather's cattle ranch is buried beneath tracts of summer homes and ski chalets.

Down in southern Arizona, abandoned cotton farms gather tumbleweeds; the water has been sold to the cities to fill swimming pools and artificial lakes big enough to put sailboats on. (Strangely enough, it takes as much water to cultivate one acre of crops as it does one acre of housing.) In the Grand Canyon, the legendary Colorado River is turned on and off like a bathroom tap to meet the changing power demands of Phoenix and Los Angeles.

Many Southwesterners are more than a little ambiguous about all this change. We wonder what it will do to the land and how it will affect the traditional communities people created by working the earth. Photographs of the remote Pueblo towns of Walpi and Taos evoke feelings of time's endlessness, but those new TV antennas at the other villages should make us wonder about the fate of Indian cultures in the hands of a generation raised on sitcoms and soap operas. Can tribal leaders guide their people across the perilous bridges of cultural transition? And what about our beleaguered farming communities? Will they be able to stop the loss of their water rights to urban users and keep their way of life intact?

The dusty bones of Father Kino recall the Southwest's Spanish and Mexican past, a time when people moved across the land unimpeded by borders. That legacy is everywhere, an unavoidable reminder that our fate is bound to the 100 million Hispanics who share this continent with us.

There is also something important about the Southwest revealed in the faces of people whose portraits are included in this collection. Here are Indian artists of world renown such as R. C. Gorman, Charles Loloma, Robert Draper, Fred Kabotie, Beatien Yazz, and Harrison Begay. Peter MacDonald and Abbott Sekaquaptewa are Indian politicians. Don Talayesva was the Sun Chief of Old Oraibi. The great writer Frank Waters is shown relaxing at home, as is the introspective dean of Southwestern photographers, Laura Gilpin. Bates Wilson was the founder of Canyonlands National Park and remains a legend in southern Utah. Georgie White Clark is, perhaps, the greatest of the commercial river runners. Environmentalist Hildegard Hamilton's photographs, along with those of her husband, were presented to Congress for the protection of Canyonlands. The Sonoran environment is a hostile place for most, but the grand old man of the desert, Tucson's Julian Hayden, could not live anywhere else.

With this book, Marc Gaede, along with David Lavender, asks us to wonder where the rush to our cities will really lead us. Perhaps it is not the artist's job to provide an answer, but these splendid photographs certainly raise the issues and invite us all to become more involved in making decisions about how much of the region's uniqueness and integrity should be preserved.

THE ENDURING SOUTHWEST

David Lavender

3. Shiprock, New Mexico 1975

The Waves of Change

The small gray chapel, surrounded by prickly desert scrub, stands almost unnoticed beside the dirt road leading toward Arivaipa Creek's magnificent redrock wilderness. Between the top of the building's yellow front door and the simple white cross on the peaked roof a white-lettered sign reads, "Salazar Family Church."

Finding the door unlocked, my wife and I went in, though we had no connection with the family. The single room held a few rows of wooden pews and a small altar decorated with painted figurines and artificial flowers. Presumably mass is held here on some Sundays when a priest is available, but mostly, I felt, the sanctuary is used for life's special occasions. Baptisms. Weddings. Funerals. And the door remains unlocked in order that any Salazar who so desires may sit a moment in the pews before the altar and contemplate, in the dusky coolness, the import of these ever-repeated rites of passage.

Subdued by the quietness, we moved back into the glaring Arizona sunlight. To the southwest was the shaggy hump of the Galiuro Mountains; to the northeast, the granitic spires of the Santa Teresas. Closer by, uprooted trees, tangles of driftwood, and clumps of boulders showed where a flash flood had thundered past the year before.

It is believed that Coronado's exploring expedition marched near here on its way north four and a half centuries ago. The land then must have looked much as it does now – wild, rough, lonesome.

"I suppose," my wife said, "that if people want – need – a church in a place like this they have to build it themselves."

I agreed. Then another thought came, tinged with a sense of loss. The Salazars have been cattlemen for many decades. This small, gray, isolated church is an emblem of their continuity, their attachment to place, where one generation flows easily into the next.

Such spots, where a person could feel himself flowing along a steady continuum of time in unrestricted space were once common in the Southwest. Now, however, the region's space and time are being increasingly fragmented, so it seems, by headlong urbanism and by the tentacles that draw sustenance out of the land for the cities.

Concrete plugs choke the distant canyons. Concrete ditches wind around pink promontories and thrust across tawny deserts. Great swatches of alluvial soil, rich in nutrients washed out of the mountains by eons of summer cloudbursts, are lost now under sterile layers of parking lots and circling subdivisions. Freeways hold their grades by slicing through mountains half as old as time and riding across gorges on untold yards of fill. Power lines are even more disdainful of the terrain, the wires between the robotlike towers dipping as gracefully as a swallow in flight and glowing, sometimes, cherry-red in the sunset.

With these developments have come not just miles of table-flat cottonfields, odorous livestock feed lots, and hurtling, slabsided trucks. Not just luxurious resorts tucked in among boulders at the feet of the mountains, and double-jointed cranes lifting the high-rise hearts of the Sun Belt cities steadily upward. There are also hosts of small peripheral changes that no one ever contemplated.

For instance, the bottom of the Grand Canyon. On torrid days when demands for power to activate air conditioners soar in south and central Arizona, extra amounts of water are sent plunging through the turbines at far-off Glen Canyon Dam on the Colorado River. Exactly as foreseen. But. The hotter the day, the higher stream levels rise in Marble Gorge and the rest of the canyon below the dam. Then, as demands for energy slack off at night and the turbines are shut to conserve water, down the levels go. Because of these fluctuations, river runners often awake in the morning to find their rafts and boats either stranded high and dry on the sand, or floating in deep water at the end of their tie ropes. As the crews make adjustments, they complain mildly. Yet most of them would not be there if the giant concrete plug did not control, as a mere incident in the storing of water and the generation of electricity, the far more violent fluctuations of earlier times – surging floods in the spring, shrunken trickles during periods of drought. Because river flows have been leveled off, relatively speaking, as many as 15,000 vacationists can now anticipate finishing, in high style, runs that were once limited to handfuls of opportunistic adventurers.

Fifteen thousand pairs of trampling feet per annum have, of course, brought noticeable – and uncontemplated – changes to camp sites and adjacent trails. The main change to the environment, however, lies in the altered nature of the water. Most of the red silt that thickened the old river now settles out in Lake Powell, behind Glen Canyon Dam. A cold, translucent pale green fluid now comes from the turbines. Little material remains in it to rebuild the soft sandbars, beloved by campers, that are slowly eroding away. Completely gone are the monumental cliffs of driftwood three to four hundred yards long and dozens of feet thick, which the early river runners set afire to watch the spectacular blazes. Streamside vegetation, along with the insects, reptiles, and birds that inhabit the vegetation, is also changing now that floods no longer ravage the banks. Native fishes, some found only in the Grand Canyon – the Colorado squawfish, the humpbacked chub, and the bonytailed chub – have become endangered species. Trout, bass, and other game fish (they were once stocked but that interference with nature has been ended) now flourish in the icy currents. Because of human insistence on change, even so prodigious a geologic feature as the bottom of the Grand Canyon does not look quite as it did when Coronado's lieutenant, Garciá López de Cárdenas and his men first sighted it from the rim 450 years ago. Yet no one really intended such a consequence. As for Glen Canyon and dozens of other reservoir sites, they have disappeared completely.

And the flow of the freeways! The reverberation of motors on Interstate 15 between the gargantuan walls of the lower gorge of the Virgin River in Arizona's far northwestern corner would have been unimaginable only a few decades ago. So, too, the constant *zip-zap-zip* on Interstate 17 at the edge of the Black Canyon, across from the forbidding, chaparral-matted slopes of the Bradshaw Mountains. But what really amazed me came one February day on Interstate 10, just east of the scant remains of a place called Ehrenberg.

During the decades after the Civil War, Ehrenberg had been a docking stop for steamboats chuffing against the current from the Gulf of California with mountains of freight for army posts and mining camps throughout central Arizona. The loads were transferred into high-sided, high-wheeled wagons and pulled by long teams of horses and mules over the Dome Rock Mountains into a desolate valley split by Tyson Wash. The teamsters' first camp was made beside a well in the valley floor.

Thinking idly of these things, I topped out of the mountains into a view of the valley and nearly ran off the road in astonishment. Tens of thousands of recreation vehicles filled the normally blank desert almost from rim to rim. Their occupants called themselves "snowbirds" and they had fled from winter in the north to various sunny spots in Arizona. They had converged briefly here at Quartzsite – permanent population 300; normal snowbird population 25,000 – to attend a five-day rockhound swap meet. Later a county deputy sheriff estimated that 350,000 people had visited the festival, a major city that took form and then dissolved in less than a week.

And so the tidal wave of tourists and home-seekers rolls on, over the concrete ribbons, under the jet contrails and smoke plumes from generating plants, beside the canals and power lines. Bulking large in the wave's makeup are hordes of desperate, Spanish-speaking immigrants hoping to find means of staying alive in this land that had once belonged to Mexico. The Southwest is the tip of a gigantic Hispanic iceberg, stretching from southern Colorado to Argentina, and many of these people are seeking relief from socio-economic pressures through a continuous northern migration. Most drift on to other parts of the nation. Many stay, crowded into *colonias* and *barrios* from Yuma to El Paso, from Tucson to Albuquerque. They settle in wretched camps in the fertile Salt and Rio Grande valleys. And they bear almost no resemblance to the Hispanics who preceded them several centuries earlier. Neither do the snowbirds resemble the tourists who came on the crack tourist trains of the 1890s. And what of the hundreds of thousands of Anglo newcomers buying both elegant and tract homes, decorated by veritable jungles of non-indigenous plants, sustained by water artificially transported hundreds of miles via a complicated maze of canals and pumping stations. Are their roots any firmer than those of the transplanted gardens?

Islands

"Earth abides," George Stewart wrote. That it does so in America, in anything like its BG (Before Gasoline) state is in large part due to the federal government's setting aside choice sections as permanent islands in the sea of change. Legislative differences that probably won't concern most people account for the different names given these islands – Wilderness Areas, Wildlife Refuges, National Parks, National Monuments, and so on. The states, too, have established parks of varying degrees of ruggedness and, in some cases, they sponsor state monuments as well. Though it is not possible for anyone except rangers to live in these reserves, they do create for those who visit them, with nerve ends alert, a "sense of place" that can serve as a first step toward developing a lasting attachment to the southwestern lands.

Wilderness areas are the children of Congress and cannot be tampered with by executive decree. There is a paradox here: as the nation's population grew increasingly urbanized, a restive movement began to preserve small pieces of its remaining uncivilized lands. Keep out development, the cry went. No management of resources, as in national forests and Bureau of Land Management holdings. No tourist facilities, as in national parks. Just the continuance, as far as possible, of the primal conditions that are so ingrained in America's concept of itself. It is worth noting, in this connection, that one of the first extensive, decreed pieces of wild land in the world is the 500,000-acre Gila Wilderness of west-central New Mexico. A few of the more recently created areas are as small as 5,000 acres.

Prima facie evidence of wildness is absence of roads, canals, or power lines within an area. If roads do exist, they should be so old and insignificant that nature is reclaiming them. Motors are not allowed, not even chain saws for clearing trails. As yet, however, no one has figured out how to keep airplanes from racketing overhead.

There are several dozen wilderness areas in the Southwest, each preserving a characteristic bit of the region's landscape, wildlife, and vegetation. Not all are as remote as the word "wilderness" suggests. Pusch Ridge, Mt. Wrightson, and the Rincons look down on Tucson; Four Peaks and the Superstitions are sometimes murky with smog rolling out from Phoenix; the Wheeler Peak and Pecos units in New Mexico lie just beyond the back doors of Taos and Santa Fe.

Variety is almost boundless. The Paria and its even more astounding tributary, Buckskin Gulch, flow out of Utah into Arizona through such deep, narrow slots that the ribbon of sky overhead seems an illusion and one can't help feeling the way miners must feel at times: what if the immeasurable weight of the rock jaws should close like a vise while you are inside? Farther south, in central Arizona, the deep red bays and thrusting promontories of Sycamore Canyon are so striking that the area is sometimes called the unknown Little Grand Canyon. Elsewhere, forests of evergreen collect deep snows in winter and give relief from the torching sun of summer: the Blue Range Wilderness rolls in waves east from Arizona into New Mexico; trailless Cruces Basin just south of Colorado offers a forest challenge to adventurers. Still higher are alpine mountaintops where tiny flowers dot the treeless tundra: the Kachina Wilderness girdles the San Francisco Peaks north of Flagstaff and, in New Mexico's Pecos Wilderness, the vast dome of Truchas Peak catches the evening's alpenglow with such intensity that it helped, nearly four hundred years ago, to give the name Sangre de Cristo, Blood of Christ, to the whole mountain range out of which it rises.

One unexpected consequence of the preservation system has been the numbers of people it fired into venturing out of their cities in order to see for themselves the last unspoiled areas of the Southwest's forests and deserts. The very name "wilderness" jerks hikers and horsemen into motion the way a magnet stirs iron filings. Bent under new backpack frames and pinched by Vibram-soled boots that don't always fit as comfortably on the trail as they did in the outfitter's store, newly converted campers struggle into the most remote areas – for one example, the shaggy Paiute Wilderness in Arizona's gaunt northwest corner. More accessible areas become, in effect, urban parks. Still, all offer somewhere within their borders magnificent viewpoints, streamlets whispering among polished boulders, and clean trails (if the users will keep them clean) winding through sweet-smelling groves of oak or pine or aspen. In such places it is possible to believe even now that earth does abide, that, to adapt A. Starker Leopold's words, there doesn't have to be a cow on *every* hill, a road in *every* valley.

If the land needed help, so too did some of the imperiled creatures who inhabited the land. One dramatic case history of what wildlife refuges can do is provided by the tall, white whooping crane, its fierce yellow eyes glaring from a partly featherless head. By 1941, guns and the drainage of their nesting marshes had, in the words of Robert P. Allen of the Audubon Society, brought the birds, which had survived since Pleistocene times, close to the "final indignity of extinction. If anything is to save [them] it must be our doing." But doing what? In 1940 or so, only twenty-one of the hoarse-voiced birds were known to exist. These were not enough to guarantee replacement, for a female whooper lays only two eggs a year. Unless life patterns could be altered, prospects looked bleak.

One hope was to persuade sandhill cranes, gray birds not as tall as the white whoopers and famous for the leaps and bows of their mating dance, to adopt chicks of the imperiled species – a quixotic gesture, since the sandhills themselves were barely holding their own. But there was this advantage. Many sandhill cranes winter beside the Rio Grande at the Bosque del Apache National Wildlife Refuge a dozen miles south of Socorro, New Mexico, a wet oasis in the desert. Their migration to their nesting grounds is shorter and far less arduous than that of the whooping cranes. That fact alone might increase an adoptee's chances for survival.

The experiment began in 1975. Whooping crane eggs were put in the nests of sandhill cranes. As fall approached, watchers at the Bosque grew nervous. Had the gray sandhill females accepted the white chicks? If so, would the young whoopers follow their foster parents when migration time arrived? Or would instinct drive them back into the hopeless pattern of their own dying species? . . . The effort succeeded. Dozens of whoopers winter in New Mexico now. Other refuges had also attracted adoptees, so that today the world population of whooping cranes numbers well over one hundred. Life will endure – if given a fighting chance.

Additional refuges – Havasu, Cibola, Imperial – have been set aside on the lower reaches of the Southwest's other great river, the Colorado, where dams back water up into twisting side channels, marshes, and mudflat deltas. As at Bosque del Apache, desert and riparian environments interfinger curiously, so that jackrabbits and roadrunner exist side by side with water-loving bitterns and ducks.

East of the river is the American extension of Mexico's Sonoran Desert – a sun-incinerated sprawl of wide, sere valley bottoms broken by thin ridges of jagged mountain ranges whose reddish volcanic rock looks as if it had been taken belatedly from its baking oven and cast aside as over-cooked. On a July day when the molten sun is sucking the last threads of moisture from air and soil, it seems that only the most primitive of crawling things could live there. And yet two enormous wildlife refuges have been established in the region – Cabeza Prieta, its 940,000 acres bordered on the south by Mexico, and, fifty or so miles farther north, the Kofa tract, its sawtoothed crest as spectacular as that of any desert range in America.

Both tracts are known best for the desert bighorn sheep they protect. For the sake of those nimble, handsome, sure-footed animals, wells have been dug and pipes run to inaccessible seeps whose water they drain, drop by drop, into cement tanks. Other life exists there, too – swift, pronghorned antelope, wild burros that would take over the waterholes if they weren't fenced away (the sheep and antelope can leap the barriers), reptiles and birds, toads and flowers, all showing clearly how opportunistic evolution can be in adapting to the harshest of environments. The kangaroo rat, Rose Houk writes, metabolizes water from the seeds it eats and uses its large nasal cavities for absorbing moisture from the air it breathes. The spadefoot toad has spurs on its hind legs, which enable it, when sitting on its rear and squirming and pushing with its front feet, to dig deep into the earth – as much as two feet – as summer's heat increases. It then lies dormant until the next rains revive it, whereupon it emerges with a great clamor of love, for its sun-threatened mating season is necessarily short.

More familiar to most travelers than wilderness areas or wildlife refuges are national parks, also created by acts of Congress. The wonders embraced by the parks of the Southwest are, in general, colossal and gaudy. Overwhelmed by them, viewers tend to be satisfied, first, with looking, and then taking photographs they hope will somehow convey the feelings they experienced as they gazed. The park service fosters these quick encounters. Paved roads and short trails lead to superlative and often crowded overviews. Yet it is very easy to be more private and more in tune with what is being saved. Simply go out before dawn, which most visitors are reluctant to do. Surrounded by such a stillness that you actually try to breathe more softly, you can watch undistracted as the rising sun, in its daily reenactment of Genesis, gives form and color to spires and cliffs and bottomless abysses.

Or, by venturing a little way from the main gathering points, you can, in every park, find remote trails that lead to delicious side canyons. There are hills to hike, crags to climb, and promontories where you can sit with your back against a warm rock while clouds and ravens – sometimes an eagle – float overhead. Listen. Listen. The Grand Canyon, said John Wesley Powell, "is the land of music." A century later, the French composer, Olivier Massiaen, heard similar resonances in Utah's Bryce and Zion canyons. From that came his contemporary, iridescent *Des Canyons aux Étoiles*, "From the Canyons to the Stars." "A many colored harmonization of chords," he said of the Zion section of the deeply religious symphony. "Play orange-red," he wrote on the score in order to help his musicians fully grasp the passage on Bryce.

One wonders, after hearing such a symphony, what some other young musician might make of the Petrified Forest's maze of rounded clay hills, their bands of color shading from mulberry to pale rust, from blue to livid gray, enlivened here and there in unexpected places, by bejeweled fossil logs. And what of the long limestone fin of the Guadalupe Mountains that rises like a crash of tympani and cymbals out of the desolate Chihuahuan Desert east of El Paso, Texas, the crescendo abruptly interspersed, now and then, with softer melodies telling of moments of peace in hidden canyons where the leaves of undesertlike maples and oaks turn to flame in the autumn?

National monuments spring into being through presidential proclamation. They stand guard over wondrous landforms such as the delicate, crescent ridgetops of sand dunes in Colorado and New Mexico, and awesome spans of stone in Utah, most particularly Rainbow Natural Bridge on the remote, stone-pleated slopes of Navajo Mountain.

National monuments also protect exotic vegetation. Just east of the Cabeza Prieta Refuge, Organ Pipe Cactus National Monument spreads its shelter over the only region in the United States where those bizarre plants grow, one of 150 or so species of cacti in the Southwest. The organ pipe sends up, from a single base, clumps of nearly perpendicular stems that resemble, in some people's minds, the pipes of a church organ – hence the name. Sometimes the pleated stems, which expand to store water after every rainfall, stand as tall as fifteen feet. The flowers, a pinkish lavender, grow on the ridges of the pleats and on the tips of the stems and bloom at night. Their fruit, like that of the giant saguaro cactus, furnishes food for the Papago Indians, whose reservation, second largest and perhaps the most poverty-stricken in the United States, joins the eastern side of the monument. From there it stretches out almost far enough to touch another guardian of cacti, the west section of Saguaro National Monument on the outskirts of Tucson.

There is a magnificent imperturbability about mature saguaros. They grow dozens of feet tall, weigh several tons, and almost invariably stand, as do the giant sequoias of California's Sierra Nevada Mountains, absolutely erect on a shallow, widespread root system. (You don't lean successfully when you weigh so much.) Their candelabra branches also try to grow vertically, parallel to the trunk, though now and then you'll see one that curls like a ram's horn. They flourish on *bajadas*, those detrital outwashes from mountain canyons; they bristle stiffly on steep hillsides, and march like gendarmes along the ridges. Their waxy white, trumpet-shaped flowers, night bloomers like those of the organ pipe cactus, produce a plump red "pear" filled with myriads of black seeds.

There have to be myriads. Birds, insects, and rodents devour the seeds ravenously. Those that escape uneaten will produce progeny only if the temperature and moisture conditions are propitious. Cattle trample and eat many of the young plants that do take root. Tract developments absorb more and more of the saguaros' favored areas. Tucson is fortunate, indeed, that in 1934 the federal government established two units east and west of the city where these aristocratic symbols of the Southwest can be preserved.

Other national monuments recall human history. Several embrace Indian ruins. Some of the remnants sprawl across flat surfaces: Aztec and the Salinas group in New Mexico; Casa Grande and Waputki in Arizona. A few perch on canyon ledges or on ridge tops: Walnut Creek and Tuzigoot, Arizona. Favored by tourists are those tucked into caves—a stunning variety: those in Canyon de Chelly; the spectacular triple sites of Navajo National Monument; Tonto, guarded by dragoons of saguaros; multistoried Chacoan cities, to give only a partial list.

The Spanish *entradas* into what is now the United States are also honored. Most of those pioneering incursions followed the Mexican Highlands, a broad uplift that pushes north out of Sonora between the Sonoran and Chihuahuan deserts. Because altitude brings increased moisture, living streams wind through the highlands. The low divide between those flowing south and those drifting north lies approximately along the present international border. Ancient trade trails crossed this divide from one valley to another, and when Europeans arrived, they followed the same routes.

The Coronado National Memorial, close to the border, overlooks the long, wide San Pedro Valley that led luckless Francisco Vásquez de Coronado to the Gila during his vain effort to find the seven legendary cities of golden Cibola. Farther west is the parallel valley of the Santa Cruz, highway of the missionaries. There the famed Jesuit, Eusebio Francisco Kino, began his work in the late 1600s. Since then, weather, time, marauding Apaches, and angry Mexican revolutionists have made ruins of many of the laboriously constructed edifices that were built on the sites he selected. Cocospera in Sonora and Guevavi in Arizona are two mute, unhappy examples. No national accolade signals their decay.

Better fortune has attended Tumacacori, eighteen miles north of Nogales. By 1908, the compound was being used by miners and cattlemen as a parking lot for their wagons and a corral for their livestock. That ended when the National Park Service acquired the ten acres surrounding the collapsing structures. Wisely, those in charge of restoration left the ambitious bell tower exactly as the Spanish had left it – unfinished. The facade, though, has been refurbished. It, a cool patio, and a fine museum, all enlivened each year by a colorful Indian festival, remind us of the initial commingling of cultures that still brings a rich flavor to the yet unhomogenized Southwest.

Far to the northeast, a little short of the sagging Continental Divide in New Mexico, another Spanish record is carved into a snout of gray rock two hundred feet high that thrusts out from a bluff visible for miles. At the base of the cliff a pool of water invites camping and a smooth face of stone invites inscriptions. *Paso por aqui* . . . (There passed by here . . .) they wrote with their dagger points and added names and dates. Inscription Rock, as the register is called, dates from Juan de Oñate in 1605.

Still farther east loom the ridgetop ruins of Cicuyé. (We call the place Pecos.) Gateway to the plains, it was the largest of the hundred or so occupied pueblos that existed in the Southwest when Coronado went through in 1541. Years later, when the Spanish colonized New Mexico, Pecos became one of their prizes. Not because of its setting, with the white peaks of the Sangre de Cristo Mountains rising in the north and the ruddy cliffs of Gallisteo Mesa forming a barricade to the west, but because it stood astride a main trade route linking Santa Fe to the Great Plains. During the following centuries – Pecos was not abandoned until 1838 – Spanish missionaries built four churches there, in sequence. The massive, roofless adobe walls of the third are the ones we see today. Here, indeed, was continuity, and we can still feel its strength as we look at what was achieved.

National monuments also memorialize American Indian traders. On the north side of the Arkansas River in Colorado, within sight of the Front Range of the Rockies, is reconstructed Bent's Fort. It was the hub of an empire. The Bent brothers and their partner, Ceran St. Vrain, also had stores in Taos. Their employees, often packing kegs of fiery grain alcohol with them, followed the nomadic Indians of the Plains from camp to camp, buying buffalo robes. Clerks at the fort swapped knives, cloth, powder, lead, traps, and more alcohol for beaver fur that bewhiskered mountainmen brought down from the high country.

But is Bent's Fort, way out at the edge of the Plains, an integral part of the Southwest? In the web of history, if not of geography, it is. General Stephen Watts Kearny's army used Bent's Fort as its jumping-off place for the conquest of the Mexican Northwest, our Southwest, in 1846. And this. As you leave the fort, headed west, you see, standing apart from the main line of the Rockies, two striking conical peaks. Indians called them Huajatolla, Breasts of the World, an allusion to the nourishment all life receives from Mother Earth. American pioneers on the mountain branch of the Santa Fe Trail, however, called the pair the Spanish Peaks, outliers of an exotic region whose customs, food, and clothing proved so entrancing that they still survive today's seas of change.

The characteristics of another kind of Indian trade are preserved at Hubbell's Trading Post, founded in 1878 at Ganado, Arizona, in the Navajo Nation. Here one finds an authentic store where Indians still buy and sell in the old ways. Navajo women weave their rugs as they have ever since learning the art from the Pueblo Indians. And Lorenzo Hubbell's home stands nearby, opulently furnished as if still ready to welcome guests and show them, at a handsomely set table, that American civilization had at last penetrated one of the most remote parts of the Southwest.

Those other tamers of the land, the Mormons, are honored at Pipe Spring National Monument, standing at the tip of a red promontory thrusting southward from the bold Vermilion Cliffs in northern Arizona. A pair of two-story stone buildings face each other across a narrow courtyard. Massive wooden gates bar the entries. Erected originally to check raiding Navajos, the fortress was completed after peace had been achieved. So Pipe Spring became a ranch headquarters, sending most of its cheese and butter and some of its beef to workers building the lean, white Temple of the Church of Jesus Christ of Latter Day Saints in St. George, the first one completed in Utah.

Later, Pipe Spring served as a rendezvous for wagon trains of Mormons being sent south to colonize in eastern Arizona. When newlyweds began returning from the new towns to St. George to have their weddings sealed in the temple, the way became known as the Honeymoon Trail, and Pipe Spring's shade trees and cool water were yearned for as the finest rest stop on the long road. A covered-wagon tourist excursion down the bone-shaking Hurricane Cliffs still keeps memories of that famous trip alive.

Another set of barriers to the inflow of immigrants are the Indian reservations. Tourists and Southwesterners alike delight in them: the Hopi towns perched on narrow fingers of yellow-brown mesas; the long red distances and fantastic buttes of Navajoland; the fragrance of grass in trading posts where Papago baskets are sold. The Hualapi's canyon-seamed, pinyon-blanketed highlands. The many-tiered pueblos: Acoma, atop its cliffs; Isleta below Albuquerque, the smell of crusty bread floating from the dome-shaped, outdoor ovens; stout Taos and its white-shrouded inhabitants. A bitter paradox prevails: While Indian culture is being corroded by the worst elements of white society, creative energies are released and have soared high. Drunk Indians fight in the streets of Gallup, wreck their pickup trucks on the road to Flagstaff, pass out soddenly in vacant lots in Page. Simultaneously, their cultural centers and the homes of their fellow tribesmen display jewelry, ceramics, textiles, carvings, and, more recently, paintings that have brought the artists international renown. Meanwhile, Indian leaders struggle to create jobs on tribal farms, in lumber mills, oilfields, and resorts. Another goal is to end exploitation of Indian coal, gas, oil, and uranium by outside interests that pay minimal prices for what they drain out of the reservations.

What will eventually develop is, at the moment, unpredictable. But for the time being, at least, the enclaves remain in the hands of the Indians, vulnerable, yes, but still one of the Southwest's most enduring examples of continuity in a land of accelerating change.

Many spots of unspoiled countryside capable of laying a spell on a person still exist outside the government-created reserves, of course. Each viewer will have his or her own favorite. It may be the birth of light in a desert valley. First, as the star glitter begins to fade, a thin silver radiance outlines the castellated mountain ridges in the east. Slowly, the glow tightens into a hard semicircle. A crown of rays thrusts like bayonets around an intervening turret. Only the smallest of breezes stirs the limber branches of the creosote bushes. Out of the breathlessness, the sunburst roars, lacquering the miles of space with gold that too soon will fade into monotones drained of life by waves of heat.

At such times preferences may turn to the cool, stately forests of ponderosa pine along Arizona's Mogollon Rim. Or to the great buttresses and bays of Utah's Arch Canyon, cutting deeply back into the grassy meadows and aspens of Elk Ridge, one more vivid example of the magic that aridity and flash floods can bring to a geologically young uplift.

For the sake of adventure you might, if your shoes are stout, try hiking across the Malpais of black lava just beyond the Continental Divide east of Inscription Rock in New Mexico. I know of no easier place to get lost, to feel the instinctive dread of hostile spirits stalking you unseen than in that jumble of knife-edged boulders, screened here and there by tortured pines and crisscrossed with deep, raw trenches left by collapsed tubes through which molten magma once flowed and which now shelter, paradoxically, smears of ice that do not melt throughout the year.

Another adventure is prowling through the pilfered remnants of mining-camp ghost towns, hunting for whatever is left to find, from sun-purpled glass to rusty, nineteenth-century iron artifacts. If you want actual treasure, you can try, as many do, to find the Lost Dutchman gold mine near the stiff upright of Weaver's Needle in the Superstition Mountains. That failing, there is the cache of loot the Apache war chief, Victorio, supposedly hid somewhere in the stark Organ Mountains back of Las Cruces, New Mexico.

A more rewarding search, although you are not allowed to remove your discoveries from their settings, is for Indian rock art. Thousands of those pictures are scattered throughout the Southwest – throughout many parts of the world, for that matter. Some are painted on the surface of the rock. More are pecked into it with percussion stones. Most can be culturally identified by style and subject portrayal. Many go far back into prehistory, though occasionally you will stumble onto pieces whose subject content shows their modernity. Smooth canyon walls provide "canvases," especially those places stained with dark desert varnish that emphasizes the lineaments of whatever is cut through it into the softly colored stone beneath. The walls of sheltered alcoves attracted some artists. Talus boulders suffice for others. A site may contain only one or two pictographs or petroglyphs – or it may be crowded with scores of jumbled figures, revealing different cultures, stratified through time.

The Great Gallery, with its haunting renditions of weird long-robed anthropomorphs, almost life-sized, is a prized feature of Horseshoe Canyon, a detached unit northwest of the main body of Canyonlands National Park, Utah. Other anthropomorphs, distinguished by bulging eyes, antennae, misshapen heads, or grotesquely squared shoulders appear at more sites than can be conveniently listed. Abstract art is also common: squizzles, zigzags, concentric circles, and the like. Even more abundant are recognizable portrayals, some only inches tall, of pregnant-looking sheep, deer, snakes, lizards, bears, and human beings. Prints of life-sized hands, often painted white but also incised into the rock, are frequently associated with the other types of drawings and carvings.

Taken together, it is a vast enigma. People were here. People with vivid imaginations and strong creative impulses. They were expressing something. But what?

It is easier to say what rock art isn't rather than to define what it may be. It is not mere doodling. It is not an attempt by prehistoric Indians to record, by means of unearthly anthropomorphs, visits by strange beings from outer space. In the opinion of trained archeologists, it is not a universal form of Indian writing, comparable to sign language, that was invented to make communication possible between tribes speaking a medley of tongues. And it certainly isn't, as one determined explicator from St. George, Utah, tries to prove, a system of writings and maps left by Celtic people who migrated to America long before Columbus.

Like all art, rock art arises out of basic cultural concepts. Shamanistic symbols, magic, rituals, a belief in animal helpers and in souls moving into states of consciousness ordinarily invisible – all these concepts and more are probably involved. An unusual painting is the thirteen-foot-long mural of a terraced pueblo with two exaggerated T-shaped doorways beside a natural arch where water flows from a hole in the top during heavy rains. It is not associated with a major ruin, and its massive size – one of the largest contained prehistoric murals in the Western Hemisphere – suggests a spiritual and emotional expression of the highest order. Beyond such suggestions, the ground grows boggy except perhaps for the highly trained anthropologist, for we inevitably project our own cultural biases onto what we are seeing. Still, it is a unique experience to place your own palm on one of those ancient handprints, whether painted on or pecked into the rock, feel the gritty sandstone, and know that you are making contact across hundreds, perhaps thousands, of years with other sentient humans who roamed across this same land, who saw it with totally different eyes, and were trying to leave some kind of record about their relationship with it.

For a closer contact with the past, there is Chimayó, a cottonwood-shaded community of Hispanic farmers and weavers who mingle easily with woodcarvers from neighboring Cordova. The towns lie quietly in the foothills of the Sangre de Cristo Mountains, a few miles east of the Santa Fe – Taos highway. Once a year, the people of Chimayó produce a mock battle between costumed, make-believe Moors and medieval Christian warriors. The jam of spectators on foot and in cars, on horses and donkeys, is mind-staggering. Gaping Anglos add their mix to the kaleidoscope. A festival queen is crowned, American-style, on the flat bed of a big truck. A rock band overpowers even the whoops of the spectators and the shouts of vendors selling food from improvised booths.

The battle takes place within a fenced field. There is no grandstand; everyone remains on foot or horseback while a narrator explains, in amplified Spanish, what is going on. Squads of horsemen line up facing each other and then charge. Armor gleams; it is some gilded substance that is supposed to look like steel. Pennants wave; capes billow. Lances dip; wooden swords flail. The melee represents the climactic battle at Granada when Christian forces drove the infidel Moors from Spain in 1492. Each year the Christians win, of course—and have ever since Juan de Oñate's colonists brought their version of the pageant to New Mexico in 1598.

From there I like to go, whenever I can, to the high north-facing rim of Mesa Verde, in Colorado, where the world drops away so abruptly that the void grabs your breath. Southward, the land slides more quietly toward the distant, curiously weathered volcanic neck of Shiprock in the New Mexico part of the Navajo Reservation. Frequently these days, the winged rock's soaring lines are blurred or even rendered invisible by murk from the chimneys of a nearby power plant. In between Shiprock and the north rim of Mesa Verde are hundreds of unseen Anasazi Indian ruins of many shapes and sizes, either crumbling into the earth of the mesatop or standing like broken fortresses in various caves along the canyon walls. The dry wind whispers: these are the remains of a civilization whose roots withered about A.D. 1300 because of lack of water and complications associated with that lack.

To the northeast, mountain ranges rise into the blueness, the La Platas first and then, dimmer in the distance, the San Juans—20,000 square miles of peaks and plateaus drained by deep canyons debouching into broad river valleys. Geologically, the San Juans have been hard-used: rumpled by old collisions between floating continental plates, worn down, raised again, smothered under lava and volcanic ash, split by fissures, carved and recarved by the ebb and flow of ice sheets. Hot mineral solutions bubbling up through the mountains' veins overflowed and left splotches of red and yellow on the elephant-hide gray of the high country's volcanic hood. Tundra adds collars of bright green. Below the collars are jackets of dark spruce fringed with beautiful aspen groves and flower-spangled meadows beloved by sheepmen. Below grove and meadow lie red and tan sedimentary layers of the sort associated with the redrock country in the less lofty parts of the Southwest. "The resulting ensemble," geographer Mel Griffiths declares flatly, "present one of the most colorful ranges on the continent."

Where once the Indians hunted and the mountain men trapped, the miners moved in. Subsequently, the mineral veins of the San Juan region produced about $725 million worth of gold, silver, copper, lead, and zinc – a tidy sum back in the days when a dollar amounted to something. Because of that wealth, small towns sprang up in nearly every one of the San Juans' magnificent, U-shaped, glacial-carved valleys. Little narrow-gauge railroads, huffing and chuffing mightily, carried supplies to the towns. From the towns, the materials were forwarded to mines still higher in the mountains by mule trains, high-sided freight wagons, and chasm-leaping tramways. Ore was brought back down the slopes in the same manner.

After the hey-day of mining faded, these appurtenances became tourist delights. Flatlanders love to wander through the quaint towns and scour the collapsing mill and mine buildings for souvenirs. Backpackers use the old mule trails, while sightseeing four-wheel-drive vans follow the rough old wagon roads over the high passes. Ski lifts have been modeled after the now-obsolete ore tramways. One narrow-gauge railroad still performs daily runs for tourists, in winter as far up the Animas Canyon from Durango as snow conditions allow and in summer, all the way to the once-rowdy town of Silverton.

The San Juans' most valuable export, though it does the mountain region itself little monetary good, is water. Those peaks vault high. Thirteen of them are 14,000 or more feet in elevation. They force winter clouds moving in from the Pacific to slide upward, a shift that increases the chill and condenses the moisture they carry into several trillion snowflakes. Drifts pile high. Avalanches roar. As soon as the spring melt begins, glittering streams leap down into the valleys, grow turbid, and coil on toward the sea.

They never quite make it. The Continental Divide, which wanders through the choppy peaks of the range, splits the pour-off between two of the Southwest's three great river systems, the Colorado and the Rio Grande. (The much smaller Salt-Gila-Verde watershed is the third.) Whatever water does not evaporate or sink into the soil is stored in huge reservoirs – millions of acre feet of it – to be used for making electricity and providing drinking, sewage, and irrigating water for the proliferating urban sprawl and megafarms of the Sun Belt.

These are the spots – the ones within reach of water's magic – where the confusions of change do run unbridled. When you are swept up by their energy, they seem overpowering. But from rims like the one in Mesa Verde you sense how circumscribed – and narcissistic – the new cities still are. In the islands between them, earth abides, offering, as does the Salazar family chapel beside Arivaipa Creek, sanctuaries for the heart. There the pulse of time still beats with its old, slow rhythms, and the blueness of space remains an emblem of the continuity that is beyond reach, at least for a while, of the frettings called development and change.

A PHOTOGRAPHER'S NOTES

Marc Gaede

To the southwestern landscape photographer, more civilization means less art. As the land fills with subdivisions and the horizons clot with power poles, the artist is increasingly restricted to public parks and protected monuments. The trouble is, Mesa Verde, the Grand Canyon, and El Morro do not speak for the whole region. What the human sprawl is destroying in the Southwest – in fact what it has already destroyed over much of the continent – is the intangible feel and flavor of unique cultures imposed on unique geographies. With this collection, I have tried to capture something that will arouse the peculiar sensations of the Southwest. It is my way of contending against the elements of change.

The most difficult area is New Mexico, which has never been noted for its spectacular land forms. Charles F. Lummis described the state in three words: "sun, silence, and adobe." If he saw it now he might change that description to "freeways, satellite dishes, and trailers." The setting, for example, of Ansel Adams's most famous photograph, "Moonrise Over Hernandez," is now almost obscured by industrial clutter. What Adams saw was the gentle, breath-taking sight of the moon illuminating a small Hispanic church and the graveyard beside it at the foot of the snow-capped Sangre de Cristo Mountains. Here's what he would see now: The church has a shiny new metal roof; a heavy construction and equipment yard encircled by galvanized fencing is pushed up against the graveyard; amongst discarded automobile bodies squats a metal industrial building surrounded by scattered mobile homes. Taos and Santa Fe may regulate their development but the rest of New Mexico builds what it wants, where it wants. Lummis's sun endures but the adobe is crumbling, and the silence is shattered. Only old photographs and paintings show us what it was like.

In Arizona, one of the fastest-growing areas of the country, the cities of Tucson and Phoenix almost touch in a sea of ranchettes. New freeways will take you anywhere you want to go, but are often impossible to exit at points of interest. Here, more than anyplace else in the Southwest, photographic composition can be entirely determined by things you *don't* want in the picture. I recall the afternoon I was trying to photograph the Mohawk Mountains in the southern part of the state. After struggling with endless visual obstacles I finally managed to get what I wanted, but not until the lens was pointed above a dirt road and a set of telephone lines, across two sets of railroad tracks, and a divided four-lane expressway, and under a towering row of 500-KV power lines. It was a desperate and frustrating situation.

The Indian reservations are changing as fast

as, or perhaps faster than, the other regions. New schools, houses, and shopping centers abound without regard to architectural good taste or their proximity to natural beauty. The serenity of the Upper Valley of Monument Valley has been destroyed by the construction of a new school. All previous buildings – Goulding's Trading Post and the Seventh-Day Adventist Hospital – were carefully sited so they didn't taint one of the country's most symbolic western environments.

Northern Mexico is not being transformed as rapidly as the rest of the Southwest, but change is happening, and my anxiety about the situation is acute. Missions, hundreds of years old, are eroding to the ground. The great haciendas of Chihuahua cave in from neglect, and the once beautiful adobe towns are drowning in a wash of modern houses and shanties, many plastered with advertisements. The people of these areas seem to think nothing of putting power lines, street lights, and signs over the most historic structures.

When I can't compose around such offensive intrusions I am faced, like all landscape photographers, with three options. I can pack up my cameras and move on, I can take it as it is, or I can retouch my prints and purge the smaller foreign objects from the image. I have no qualms about removing objectionable elements from my compositions if they are truly distracting, and if my editing is honest. I frequently remove trailers, houses, power lines, automobiles, trash, graffiti, and other nonconformities. Ansel Adams must have felt the same way when he erased the white rocks, which formed the letters "LP," from the hillside in his photograph "Winter Sunrise at Lone Pine." Even before he exposed the negative he knew that the rocks would appear in his print and he knew he was going to make them disappear with the spotting brush. The photographer who is unwilling to take these kinds of measures will eventually discover that there's not much of the landscape left to take pictures of.

Many photographers wait patiently for lighting and composition. I know of some who stand for days hoping an image appears, with frequently successful results. I don't have that kind of disposition. Not only am I inherently impetuous, I have only a limited amount of time to get things done in the field. My method of photography is to speed from one place to another to catch as many expressive moments as quickly as I can. If one place isn't productive, I move on. The process is not random, for I know my subjects well, and the image is usually in my mind before I arrive. Also, I will not waste film on a forced composition just because I am there. I must feel something for the image. For me, it is important that filtration, exposure, and development be honest to the spirit and mood of the situation. Nothing is worse, I believe, than the misuse of heavy filters, of short focal length lenses, and of exaggerated contrast, which only serve to misconvey things that need little to reveal their essence.

Photography in the field is usually a combination of rewards and frustrations. The disappointments are much more common than the successes, and to the experienced landscape photographer, this is accepted as part of the process. What follows is an account of a day I spent in March 1985, during one of my field trips from Los Angeles to Sonora, Mexico.

The day begins at 6 a.m. I'm camped beside the Colorado River near Yuma, Arizona. After exploring the junction of the Colorado and Gila rivers, I am unable to find an interesting subject to photograph. The Gila Trail once followed the river from which it got its name, and for two centuries was the gateway to California. Today there is almost nothing remaining to indicate its historic importance. I ignore the Yuma Indian Tribe's signs telling non-Indians to stay out, and poke around at will upstream. At 8 a.m. I leave the monument to the martyred Father Garces and drive my truck across the Colorado River back into Arizona. By 9 a.m. I am in the Mohawk Mountains 45 miles east of Yuma, trying to skirt the U.S. Air Force gunnery range. For two years I have been trying to capture the beautiful feeling of distance these desert peaks, back-lit by the sun, radiate in the morning. The look of this monotone desert, using black and white photography, has been a frustrating experience for me; in color it would be easy. Knowing that my main objective today is Caborca, Mexico, I realize I'll have to hurry to make the evening light.

By 10 a.m. I'm back on the pavement headed east at seventy miles an hour. My old Ford has three fuel tanks and a newly rebuilt engine. I can eat later – my two thermos bottles are full of coffee. Reading the map over the steering wheel, I see that I can save about an hour by going through the Sasabe, Mexico, crossing; that is, if there's no line for visas at the obscure border station there. Also, the road to Sasabe passes by Baboquivari Peak, and maybe I can get a shot of it. At 1 p.m. I pass Picacho Peak at eighty miles an hour. Storm clouds are building and it becomes apparent that making Caborca before dark is going to be tough.

By 2 p.m. I am frantically pumping gas into my tanks on the outskirts of Tucson. I grab a few candy bars and hit the westbound road to Sasabe. The road quickly becomes two lanes and I have to slow down; my blood pressure goes up – I know how little time is left. I have a notion about how to handle the facade of the Mission in Caborca and it will only work in the late light of afternoon. Thus, there is no chance to get anything tomorrow morning and I don't have time to wait around another day for the proper light. It's now or never, at least on this trip. As I pass Three Points the traffic thins and I open the throttle.

Passing by Baboquivari Peak, I am sort of relieved to see that the mountain is completely socked in by rain clouds. At least I don't have to make a decision about stopping. The crossing into Mexico is mercifully fast. I am probably the only person to go over today and the border guards seem pleased that somebody knows they exist. The road is now dirt and mud with many stretches covered in water from the rains. But I am really flying. I've got one eye on my watch and one eye on the road. In only 90 minutes the sun will be down. I'm driving seventy miles an hour in the spots where the road will allow it. Some of the cattle guards have lips and the truck literally sails through the air as my race with time goes on.

It's decision time again. At these speeds I risk wrecking or damaging the truck but if I slow down I won't have a prayer of making Caborca before sundown.

To hell with it. One good picture is probably worth the truck in dollars. Besides, I've been driving like a madman for six hours and don't want to give up now. Sliding around corners, through endless mudholes, shifting up and down the gears, in and out of four-wheel drive, I watch the sun dart through the clouds as it sinks nearer the horizon.

The dirt road finally connects with pavement, and then the pavement connects with Mexican Route 2. I'm headed west and the sun is right in my eyes. I can't see oncoming traffic but I can hear the roar when something speeds by and glimpse the blur through the window on my side of the truck. I've still got my foot to the floor – the speedometer says ninety. A sign says Caborca, twenty kilometers. I remember that the mission is on the far side of town. God, if I just had another ten minutes! The Ford is making funny noises. Lifters, I think – I hope. If it's rods, big trouble, big money, and another rebuilt engine.

The sun finally drops just as I enter Caborca. If I hurry, I still have a few minutes. The afterglow of sunset is just the right light for this kind of image. However, I'll never make it to the mission in time if I try to drive through town – the streets are clogged with end-of-the-day traffic. I decide to gamble and drive the perimeter.

It works! The unfamiliar roads hook up with the last brick boulevard. Suddenly, there it is, the mission, glowing beautifully in the distance. Racing, I plan my attack. I will pull up to the plaza in front of the mission, park facing traffic on the wrong side of the road. My exposure . . . let's see, ASA 200 for Tri X, f4 at 125th of a second for zone five equals f64 at 1/2 a second plus three stops for the filter gives a final exposure of sixteen seconds at f45 counting an extra stop for reciprocity. The lens will be the 12-inch Dagor, which doesn't work below 1/15th but that's okay because I'll be using my watch on the bulb shutter setting.

The light holds as I screech to a stop, sliding through a large puddle of water to the mission plaza. I park pointed toward the oncoming traffic. I jump out of the truck, run back to the camper, throw open the door, pull out my extended tripod, thrash through my many cases to find the right equipment and then sprint to a spot in front of the mission. A crowd of mystified Hispanics turn to watch the insane gringo.

That's when I see it.

Larger than life, impossibly ugly. And right smack in front of the mission's front door – a concrete septic tank the size of my truck. The good people of Caborca, justifiably proud of their beautiful mission, wanted it to have a real sewer system. And the powers that be, in a prideful gesture, decided to display the tank right out front before they put it in the ground and hooked it up.

No amount of retouching can make the tank disappear from my image. I am stunned with defeat.

Shuffling back to the road, I find the truck wheezing and shaking as it tries to run despite the fact that the ignition is off. Antifreeze squirts onto the pavement and oil burns on the manifold.

I pull into a parking lot and heat up canned beef on a propane stove for my first meal of the day. I try to understand the significance of it all.

The rain starts again. It is dark. I pack up my equipment and give the septic tank a parting gesture. As I drive off toward Magdalena, I know that the tank will end up where it deserves to be and when it does, I'll be back.

At ten that night, after filling the truck with gas, I pull into Magdalena. It's been raining here all day too and the streets are filled with water. I had already photographed Kino's remains in the crypt on the plaza two months ago, but by street light I could see nothing more of interest here. However, the mission of San Ignacio is just up the road, and it might be interesting.

It is. The light on the whitewashed facade is beautiful and soft. The exposure I make is twenty-eight minutes, the longest shot I have ever taken. Dogs and cats walk through the composition but I know they wouldn't show up in the negative as long as they keep moving. When one irreverent little cur tries to relieve himself on the facade, I pelt him with rocks until he gives up.

At 11:30 p.m. I move on. Just outside Imuris, I'm stopped by a military road block. The area is lit up by coffee cans full of burning oil. The soldiers search the truck, looking for guns, then wave me on. Beyond Imuris the road climbs into the mountains. There is snow on the ground up here and ice on the asphalt. On top, I pass by the Mission of Cocospera. Founded by Father Kino in the late 1600s, it's one of the most intriguing missions in the whole Pimería Alta region. But it's falling apart. Nature and vandals are wreaking havoc on the helpless, unprotected structure. As I wind down through the switchbacks on the other side of the mountains I pass shrines to the Virgin Mary glowing with candles lit by truckers praying for safe passage. On the outskirts of Cananea the town's brand new ambulance has been hit by the town's only train, one that carries mine ore, and there is a big commotion.

At 3:30 a.m., in Agua Prieta, I call it quits and park the camper among the big trucks on the edge of town. The thick fog is cold and clammy. I collapse in the camper and try to go to sleep fast – the truckers will be my alarm clock when they start their engines at dawn.

It's been a long, long day.

Most photographers love to talk about their gear, and thus I feel an obligation to mention what I have used to make the images in this book. I have accumulated all of my equipment by rummaging through photographic catalogues and used camera stores. Some of it is the best, and some of it isn't.

CAMERAS
8×10 Ansco
5×7 Deardorff
4×5 Wista
4×5 Graflex
2½×2¾ Pentax
2½×2¼ Hasselblad

LENSES (View Camera)
24″ Red Dot Artar
500mm Tele-Xenar
12″, 10¾″, 8¼″ Golden Dagors
135mm Symmar-S
90mm Angulon

TRIPODS
Gitzo, #3 head with three sets of legs
Leitz Tiltall

FILM DEVELOPER
D-76
HC-110

PRINT DEVELOPER
Dektol

FILTERS
3×3 or 4×4 gelatin
Wratten #8
Wratten #11
Wratten #21
Wratten #23
Wratten #25
Wratten #29
Wratten #58

PRINTING PAPER
Oriental Seagull

ENLARGER LENSES
100mm Componon-S
135mm Rodagon
640mm Rodagon

LIGHT METER
Pentax 1° Spotmeter

FILM
Kodak Plus X
Kodak Tri X

PRINTING ENLARGERS
Beseler 4×5 MCRX with Ferrante Codelite
Beseler 4×5 with condenser light source
Consolidated International C-10 8×10 fitted with a 14×14 Ferrante Codelite

IMAGES FROM THE SOUTHWEST

4. Ophir Pass, San Juan Mountains, Colorado 1985

5. Mine and tailings, Ophir, Colorado 1985

6. Corrals in snow, Lizard Head Pass, Colorado 1986

7. Old wagon and shed, Sangre De Cristo Mountains, New Mexico 1984

8. Mount Wilson Range of the San Miguel Mountains, Colorado 1986

9. Zion Canyon Overlook, Utah 1986

10. La Sal Mountains from Dead Horse Point, Utah 1985

11. Professor Valley in snow, Utah 1974

12. Goosenecks of the San Juan River, Utah 1984

13. Shiprock, New Mexico 1983

14. Agathlán, Arizona 1985

15. San Francisco Peaks, Arizona 1983

16. Spanish Peaks, Colorado 1985

17. Marble Canyon and the Colorado River, Grand Canyon, Arizona 1985

18. Junction of the Little Colorado and the Colorado rivers, Grand Canyon, Arizona 1986

19. The Nankoweap meets the Colorado River, Grand Canyon, Arizona 1985

20. Little Colorado River Gorge, Arizona 1983

21. Little Colorado River, Arizona 1976

22. Cinder hills in snow, Arizona 1978

23. Sunset Crater in snow, Arizona 1978

24. Three Sisters and hogan, Monument Valley, Utah 1984

25. Upper Valley, Monument Valley, Utah 1978

26. The Yeibichai, Monument Valley, Utah 1984

27. The Mittens, Monument Valley, Utah 1983

28. The Mittens in snow, Monument Valley, Utah 1984

29. Navajo Mountain, Utah 1986

30. The southern Hopi buttes, Arizona 1985

31. Chinde (ghost) hogan, Nitsin Valley, Arizona 1976

32. Navajo wagon and hogan, Nitsin Valley, Arizona 1976

33. Mormon house, Bluff, Utah 1985

34. Dog at Taos Pueblo, New Mexico 1974

35. Taos Pueblo, New Mexico 1974

36. Moenkopi, Arizona 1985

37. Walpi, Arizona 1978

38. Harrison Begay, Flagstaff, Arizona 1975

39. Beatien Yazz, Wide Ruins, Arizona 1984

40. Fred Kabotie, Shungopavi, Arizona 1985

41. R. C. Gorman, Taos, New Mexico 1982

42. Charles Loloma, Third Mesa, Arizona 1976

43. Vera Pooyouma, Hotevilla, Arizona 1971

44. Garnet Pavatea, Sichomovi, Arizona 1978

45. Sun Chief, Don Talayesva, Oraibi, Arizona 1973

46. Manuel Kooyahoema, Hotevilla, Arizona 1985

47. Navajo cowboys, Flying M Ranch, Arizona 1981

48. Robert Draper, Canyon de Chelly, Arizona 1984

49. Abbott Sekaquaptewa, Second Mesa, Arizona 1978

50. Peter MacDonald, Gallup, New Mexico 1982

51. Navajo petroglyphs, Rock Point, Arizona 1985

52. Hopi Clan petroglyphs, The Salt Rocks, Arizona 1985

53. Anasazi shrine, Utah 1971

54. The Great Gallery, Fremont pictographs, Barricr Canyon, Utah 1971

55. Storm over Pueblo Bonito, Chaco Canyon, New Mexico 1971

56. Doorways in Pueblo Bonito, Chaco Canyon, New Mexico 1971

57. Kin Bineola, Chaco Canyon, New Mexico 1975

58. Cliff Palace, Mesa Verde, Colorado 1976

59. Spruce Tree House, Mesa Verde, Colorado 1975

60. Canyon de Chelly, Arizona 1977

61. Canyon de Chelly, Arizona 1984

62. Horses in Canyon del Muerto, Arizona 1984

63. Antelope House, Canyon del Muerto, Arizona 1975

64. Mummy Cave, Canyon del Muerto, Arizona 1975

65. Trail to White House, Canyon de Chelly, Arizona 1978

66. White House, Canyon de Chelly, Arizona 1975

67. Burned trees, Canyon de Chelly, Arizona 1985

68. Miner's camp, Oatman, Arizona 1983

69. Colorado River and the Needle Mountains, Arizona 1985

70. Soda Lake (dry), California 1986

71. The Black Mountains, Arizona 1985

72. Baboquivari Peak, Arizona 1985

73. Bajada of the Ajo Mountains, Arizona 1985

74. Hacienda San Diego de Luis Terrazas, Chihuahua 1985

75. Franciscan church, Janos, Chihuahua 1985

76. Remains of Father Eusebio Francisco Kino, Magdalena, Sonora 1985

77. Altar of the Jesuit mission, Cocospera, Sonora 1985

78. La Purísima Concepcion de Nuestra Señora de Caborca, Sonora 1986

79. San Xavier del Bac, Arizona 1985

80. Fishermen's graves, Gulf of California 1972

81. Shipwreck, Gulf of California 1974

82. Ansel Adams and Alan Ross, Carmel, California 1977

83. Laura Gilpin, Santa Fe, New Mexico 1976

84. Julian Hayden, Tucson, Arizona 1977

85. Frank Waters, Tucson, Arizona 1985

86. Bates Wilson, Professor Valley Ranch, Utah 1973

87. Hildegard Hamilton, Flagstaff, Arizona 1978

88. Georgie White Clark, Lake Mead, Nevada 1986

89. Buster Holt, Flying M Ranch, Arizona 1978

LIST OF PHOTOGRAPHS

33. Mormon house, Bluff, Utah 1985
34. Dog at Taos Pueblo, New Mexico 1974
35. Taos Pueblo, New Mexico 1974
36. Moenkopi, Arizona 1985
37. Walpi, Arizona 1978
38. Harrison Begay, Flagstaff, Arizona 1975
39. Beatien Yazz, Wide Ruins, Arizona 1984
40. Fred Kabotie, Shungopavi, Arizona 1985
41. R. C. Gorman, Taos, New Mexico 1982
42. Charles Loloma, Third Mesa, Arizona 1976
43. Vera Pooyouma, Hotevilla, Arizona 1971
44. Garnet Pavatea, Sichomovi, Arizona 1978
45. Sun Chief, Don Talayesva, Oraibi, Arizona 1973
46. Manuel Kooyahoema, Hotevilla, Arizona 1985
47. Navajo cowboys, Flying M Ranch, Arizona 1981
48. Robert Draper, Canyon de Chelly, Arizona 1984
49. Abbott Sekaquaptewa, Second Mesa, Arizona 1978
50. Peter MacDonald, Gallup, New Mexico 1982
51. Navajo petroglyphs, Rock Point, Arizona 1985
52. Hopi Clan petroglyphs, The Salt Rocks, Arizona 1985
53. Anasazi shrine, Utah 1971
54. The Great Gallery, Fremont pictographs, Barrier Canyon, Utah 1971
55. Storm over Pueblo Bonito, Chaco Canyon, New Mexico 1971
56. Doorways in Pueblo Bonito, Chaco Canyon, New Mexico 1971
57. Kin Bineola, Chaco Canyon, New Mexico 1975
58. Cliff Palace, Mesa Verde, Colorado 1976
59. Spruce Tree House, Mesa Verde, Colorado 1975
60. Canyon de Chelly, Arizona 1977
61. Canyon de Chelly, Arizona 1984
62. Horses in Canyon del Muerto, Arizona 1984
63. Antelope House, Canyon del Muerto, Arizona 1975
64. Mummy Cave, Canyon del Muerto, Arizona 1975
65. Trail to White House, Canyon de Chelly, Arizona 1978
66. White House, Canyon de Chelly, Arizona 1975
67. Burned trees, Canyon de Chelly, Arizona 1985
68. Miner's camp, Oatman, Arizona 1983
69. Colorado River and the Needle Mountains, Arizona 1985
70. Soda Lake (dry), California 1986
71. The Black Mountains, Arizona 1985
72. Baboquivari Peak, Arizona 1985
73. Bajada of the Ajo Mountains, Arizona 1985
74. Hacienda San Diego de Luis Terrazas, Chihuahua 1985
75. Franciscan church, Janos, Chihuahua 1985
76. Remains of Father Eusebio Francisco Kino, Magdalena, Sonora 1985
77. Altar of the Jesuit mission, Cocospera, Sonora 1985
78. La Purísima Concepcion de Nuestra Señora de Caborca, Sonora 1986
79. San Xavier del Bac, Arizona 1985
80. Fishermen's graves, Gulf of California 1972
81. Shipwreck, Gulf of California 1974
82. Ansel Adams and Alan Ross, Carmel, California 1977
83. Laura Gilpin, Santa Fe, New Mexico 1976
84. Julian Hayden, Tucson, Arizona 1977
85. Frank Waters, Tucson, Arizona 1985
86. Bates Wilson, Professor Valley Ranch, Utah 1973
87. Hildegard Hamilton, Flagstaff, Arizona 1978
88. Georgie White Clark, Lake Mead, Nevada 1986
89. Buster Holt, Flying M Ranch, Arizona 1978

ACKNOWLEDGMENTS

I would like to thank all my friends and colleagues who have shared their knowledge of photography or who have given me a better understanding and appreciation of the lands and people portrayed through my cameras. In this respect, I cannot claim total credit for whatever might be significant in my images.

I should also like to thank the staff of Northland Press, especially Bruce Andresen, Linda Andrews, and Betti Arnold. Susan McDonald was extraordinary in her sensitivity to the project, and her encouragement was sustaining on every level of production. Additional appreciation is given to pressmen Jerry Weishapl and Brad Busby, and film stripper Paul Berg.

At Fabe Lithography I would like to thank photolithographer Mickey Delfiner whose expert work is unequaled. Pressman Skip Bogel conducted special press proofs to formulate ink types and analyze negative variations.

Additional thanks goes to Raymond M. Contino.

Finally, I am immeasurably grateful to Mr. and Mrs. E. Cardon Walker and Mr. and Mrs. Peter G. Wray for their generosity and loyalty for over a decade of support. Their private funding has enabled me to pursue a photographic career that would have been otherwise impossible.

—Marc Gaede

This book was edited and designed by Bill Vaughn,
and typeset in Garth Graphic by Kitty Herrin
of Arrow Graphics, Missoula, Montana.